How to get a US Bank Account for Non-US Citizen

I'd like to dedicate this book to my mom and sister

CONTENTS

CHAPTER 1 - WHY A US BANK ACCOUNT

For Small Business Owners / Entrepreneurs, to accept payment from a US Company such as Amazon, sometimes easier to use a US Bank account instead of local bank account.

If you have a lot of money, then it's probably easy for you to visit the foreign banks in your local area such as HSBC or Citibank.

The minimum deposit required to do that still higher compare with minimum deposit required to open an account at the local bank.

Unfortunately, the requirements to open a US Bank account is not very easy especially for some countries.

CHAPTER 2 -
INTRODUCTION
TO PAYONEER

Here's one of the alternative that you can do.

Payoneer is an online service where you can receive payment from your customer very easily. You can also use it to pay your employees or vendors as well. All you've got to do just Sign Up to the website and create an account.

Here's what you can do with Payoneer :

- Get paid to International Receiving Accounts (in USD, EUR, CAD, AUD, JPY, MXN)
- Expand into new MarketPlaces
- Request a Payment
- Withdraw your earnings
- Pay your VAT
- Pay your Suppliers
- Connect With Partner Ecosystem
- Access Working Capital

Payoneer can also be downloaded from Google Play for Android users and App Store for iOS users

CHAPTER 3 - REGISTER WITH PAYONEER

So the first step to get a US Bank account is by signing up an account with Payoneer.

1. Go to : Payoneer Website
2. Click on Register button on the top right side
3. Follow the instruction until finish

After the registration complete, you will receive an email with a subject "Your application to Payoneer is under review"

Once approved, you can sign-in to your account.

You can see your US Bank account by going to menu "Receive" then choose "Global Payment Service"

Under Receiving Accounts, you will see 3 Accounts with different currencies :

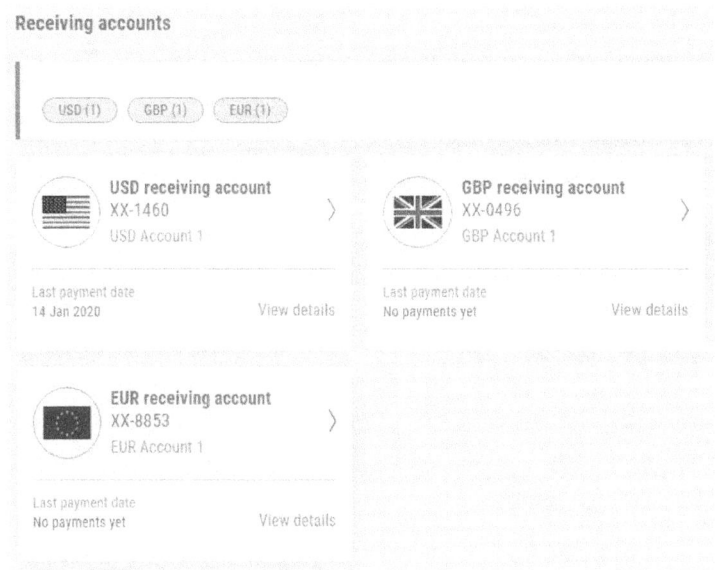

Payoneer already created 3 Accounts for you to use which are USD, GBP and EUR receiving accounts with the options to add AUD, CAD and JPY receiving accounts.

However, if you want to activate additional currencies, there will be some questions asked

* Mark the currencies you'd like to get paid in.
  - ☐ JPY

* Which marketplaces are you currently selling on?

☐ Aliexpress	☐ Amazon US	☐ Amazon JP
☐ Amazon UK	☐ Amazon EU	☐ Amazon CN
☐ Amazon Canada	☐ Amazon Australia	☐ Amazon MX
☐ Best Buy	☐ Cdiscount	☐ Ebay
☐ ePrice	☐ JD	☐ Jumia
☐ Lazada	☐ Linio	☐ Mercado Libre
☐ Newegg	☐ Priceminister	☐ Rakuten JP
☐ Rakuten US	☐ Shopee	☐ Shopify
☐ Tophatter	☐ Walmart	☐ Wish
☐ Yahoo	☐ Zalora	☐ Other

* What is your total monthly sales volume?

Select one   ▾

To see the details of your US Bank Account, click on "View details" next to "USD receiving account"

USD receiving account XX-1460
USD Account 1

 Guidelines

* Only ACH (US local bank) transfers in USD can be accepted
* Transfers must be made from a company account
* Transfers from individuals will be automatically rejected
* Wire transfers are not supported
* Transfers made from a company account owned by you cannot be accepted

Bank name	First Century Bank
Routing (ABA) Where to find	061120084
Account number Where to find	4010517681460
Account type	CHECKING
Beneficiary name Connecting to a marketplace?	▄▄▄▄▄▄▄▄▄

Share account details

Coming soon

GBP receiving account XX-0496
GBP Account 1

(i) **Guidelines**

* Only BACS and Faster Payments Service (UK local bank) transfers in GBP can be accepted
* Transfers must be made from a company bank account
* Transfers in USD will be automatically rejected
* Wire transfers are not supported

Bank name   Barclays

Sort code   231486

Account number   04440496

Beneficiary name
Connecting to a marketplace? 

Share account details

  Coming soon

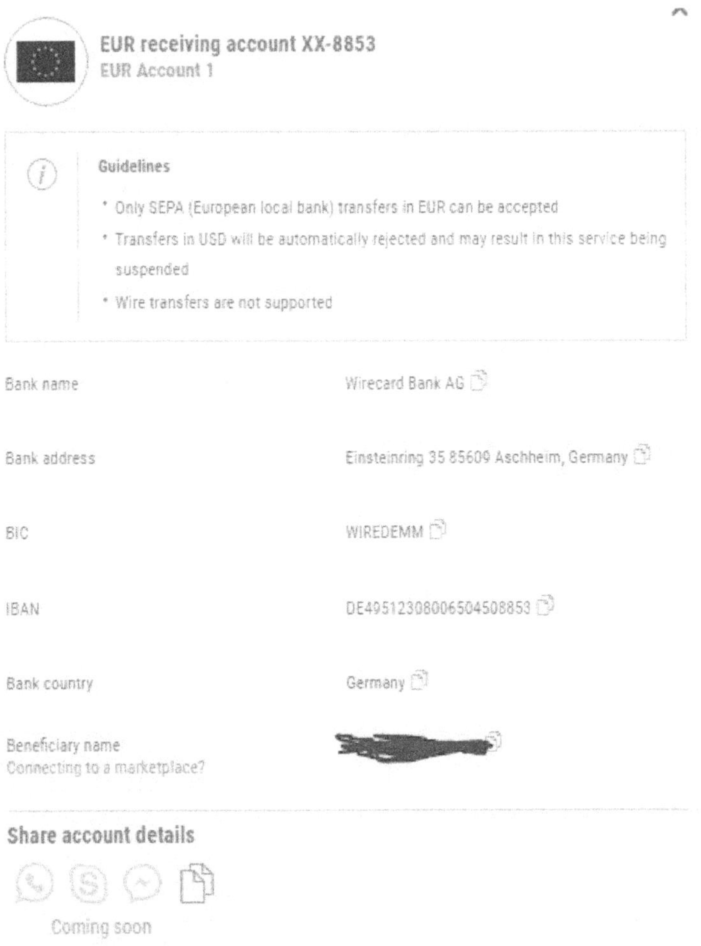

EUR receiving account XX-8853
EUR Account 1

(i) **Guidelines**

* Only SEPA (European local bank) transfers in EUR can be accepted
* Transfers in USD will be automatically rejected and may result in this service being suspended
* Wire transfers are not supported

Bank name   Wirecard Bank AG

Bank address   Einsteinring 35 85609 Aschheim, Germany

BIC   WIREDEMM

IBAN   DE49512308006504508853

Bank country   Germany

Beneficiary name
Connecting to a marketplace?

Share account details

Coming soon

That's it, now you're the owner of a US Bank Account with Euro and GBP Account as bonuses.

CHAPTER 4 - TOP-UP MONEY TO YOUR PAYONEER ACCOUNT

So the next question is how to top up your money into your Payoneer account ?

Each account has a guideline on how to receive money into that account.

For USD receiving account, here's the guidelines :

 Guidelines

* Only ACH (US local bank) transfers in USD can be accepted
* Transfers must be made from a company account
* Transfers from individuals will be automatically rejected
* Wire transfers are not supported
* Transfers made from a company account owned by you cannot be accepted

For GBP receiving account, here's the guidelines :

Guidelines

* Only BACS and Faster Payments Service (UK local bank) transfers in GBP can be accepted
* Transfers must be made from a company bank account
* Transfers in USD will be automatically rejected
* Wire transfers are not supported

For Euro receiving account, here's the guidelines :

Guidelines

* Only SEPA (European local bank) transfers in EUR can be accepted
* Transfers in USD will be automatically rejected and may result in this service being suspended
* Wire transfers are not supported

It seems a bit complicated, right ? But not really ...

Here's some ways to do that :

1. If you have an Amazon Store, you can connect your store to Payoneer and Amazon will send payments directly to your US Bank Account listed in your Payoneer account.

Opening an Amazon Store is quite simple, just go to : Amazon Website then scroll down to the bottom page and you will find this section:

Make Money with Us

Sell on Amazon

Sell Your Services on
Amazon

Sell on Amazon Business

Sell Your Apps on Amazon

Become an Affiliate

Advertise Your Products

Self-Publish with Us

› See More

Choose whichever that suits you and start your own
Amazon Store at the very low cost.
2. Refer a friend to open a Payoneer account and you
will receive $25 commision.

On your Payoneer account, go to "Activity" then
"Refer a friend". You will have the option to share
your referral link using Email, Facebook, Twitter
and LinkedIn

However, there's a prerequisite before you get the
$25 commision:

* After your friend signs up and receives 1000 USD, you'll earn 25 USD and your friend will earn 25 USD. Learn more.
By referring a friend to Payoneer, you accept our Terms & Conditions.

When your friends receive your link through Email,

Facebook, Twitter or LinkedIn, they will be redir-
ected to Sign Up page.

Once they finished signing up and received at
least USD 1,000 in payments, you and your friends
will receive the USD 25 commission within three
months.

3. Request a Payment function in menu "Receive"
then "Request a Payment"

Request a Payment

**To enable Request a Payment, you must first receive at
least 5,000.00 USD (or equivalent) via:**

The Global Payment Service, which enables you to
receive local payments from companies worldwide

Learn more >

Any of the marketplace, network, or business
platforms integrated with Payoneer

Learn more >

Still to earn: 5,000.00 USD

0.00   5,000.00

Don't worry, other than Amazon, you can find many
other companies also using Payoneer to send pay-

ments to their employees such as Teespring, Ezoic, RevenueHitz, and many more.

CHAPTER 5 - PAYONEER FEES

How much is the fee to receive money via Payoneer?

WAYS TO GET PAID

1. From Another Payoneer Customer

FREE
USD | EUR | GBP | JPY

2. Via Receiving Accounts

FREE
EUR | GBP | JPY | AUD | CAD | MXN

0-1%
USD
Fee varies by country

3. Directly from Your Customers

3%
Credit Card (all currencies)

1%
eCheck (USD)

4. Via Marketplaces & Networks

Fees set by each marketplace or
network may vary.
Please check their website for
precise rates.

WAYS TO WITHDRAW FUNDS TO YOUR BANK ACCOUNT

1. To Your Local Bank Account

UP TO 2%
ABOVE MID-MARKET RATE

2. To a Bank Account in The Same Currency

$1.50

USD

€1.50

EUR

£1.50

GBP

WAYS TO PAY

1. Pay Your Suppliers & Contractors via eCheck, credit card and local bank transfer

1%
eCHECK

3%
CREDIT CARD

1%
LOCAL BANK TRANSFER

2. Pay Your Suppliers, Contractors & Business Partners from your Payoneer Balance

FREE
TO A RECIPIENT'S PAYONEER ACCOUNT

CHAPTER 6 – WITHDRAW MONEY FROM PAYONEER

There are 2 ways to withdraw money from Payoneer:

1. Withdraw to local bank account

First, you need to add your local bank account by going to "Settings" then "Bank Accounts". You can add your local bank account up to 3 bank accounts. Then, to do the Withdraw process, go to "Withdraw" then "To Bank Account"

For USD Account, the Min Amount that you can withdraw is USD 50 and the Max Amount is USD 10,000

For EUR Account, the Min Amount that you can withdraw is EUR 40 and the Max Amount is EUR 10,000

For GBP Account, the Min Amount that you can withdraw is GBP 40 and the Max Amount is GBP 10,000

2. Payoneer Prepaid Mastercard

To apply for Payoneer Prepaid Mastercard, go to "Settings" then "Payoneer Cards"

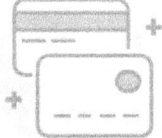

The Payoneer card. A great way to access and spend your earnings.

You'll be able to order a Payoneer card once you receive payments of 30.00 USD (or equivalent) to your account.

*Not including Make a Payment and payments from ewallets

1 Payoneer Card will be link to 1 Currency. So if you want to link all 3 Currencies, you need to order 3 Cards.

Once the card is active, your current balance for the specific currency will be transfer automatically to the card every 24 hours. So no need to do the transfer process manually.

However, there's a USD 5,000 daily transfer limit between your account and your card.

This card can be used at ATMs, in stores or online transactions that accepted MasterCard

CHAPTER 7 - INTRODUCTION TO TRANSFERWISE

Another alternative to be consider is TransferWise.

So what exactly is TransferWise ?

Basically, it's an online service to send money abroad. Their tagline is "The cheap, fast way to send money abroad."

In their website, TransferWise compare themselves to several banks such as NatWest, RBS and Barclays and they also claim to be cheaper than PayPal

Compare the costs	TransferWise	PayPal
Cost to create account	£0	£0
Monthly account fees	£0	£0
Send or pay £2000 to EUR	£7.78	£98.16
Send or pay £2000 to USD	£8.64	£92.78
Send or pay €2000 to GBP	€8.70	€90.76
Send or pay A$2000 to GBP	A$10.67	A$94.77
Receive a €2000 payment in GBP	£0	£66.47
Receive a $2000 payment in GBP	£0	£66.88
Receive a A$2000 payment in GBP	£0	£56.28

So let's start registering an Account at TransferWise

CHAPTER 8 - REGISTER WITH TRANSFERWISE

TransferWise offering Personal Account and Business Account

If you want to register for Busines Accounts, please prepare documents related to your Business such as Registration Number for your company / business.

But for this purpose, let's Sign Up for Personal Account and we can always upgrade to Business Account later

1. Go to : TransferWise Website
2. Click on "Get Started" button to start registration
3. Follow the instruction until finish

Once approved, you can login to TransferWise account.

Under "Activity" menu, you can see your balances in USD and GBP.

To see your USD Bank Account, click on the arrow next to USD sign.

You should see something like this:

Account Holder

Account number
8310367864

Wire transfer number
026073008

Bank code (SWIFT / BIC)
CMFGUS33

Routing number (ACH or ABA)
026073150

Address
TransferWise
19 W 24th Street
New York
10010
United States

To see your GBP Bank Account, click on the arrow next to GBP Sign.

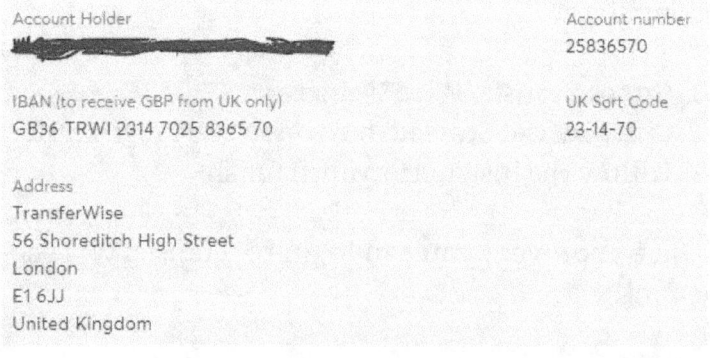

Account Holder

Account number
25836570

IBAN (to receive GBP from UK only)
GB36 TRWI 2314 7025 8365 70

UK Sort Code
23-14-70

Address
TransferWise
56 Shoreditch High Street
London
E1 6JJ
United Kingdom

According to TransferWise, "This isn't a bank account, but the unique account details we give you work in the same way when receiving money."

There's a daily and yearly limit to the account

Personal and business limits

	Personal limit	Business limit
All currencies except USD	No limit	No limit
USD limit, per transaction and per day	250,000 USD	3,000,000 USD
USD limit per year	1,000,000 USD	5,000,000 USD

Unfortunately, there's no information about the limitation for GBP Account.

If you need other currency, go to menu "Balances" then on the top left there's a button "Open a balance"

It will open a new window with a list of currencies that you can choose from such as EUR, AUD, etc

TransferWise also has a Direct Debits feature but it's still in beta phase and currently, supported only GBP and EUR accounts.

CHAPTER 9 - TOP-UP MONEY TO YOUR TRANSFERWISE ACCOUNT

TransferWise has a very easy way to top-up money into the account.

First, choose which account do we want to add the money into, the USD or GBP account.

Then, at the bottom of the Account there's an Add Button that we can click and will open a new window where we will be prompted to enter an amount that we want to add

How much do you want to add?

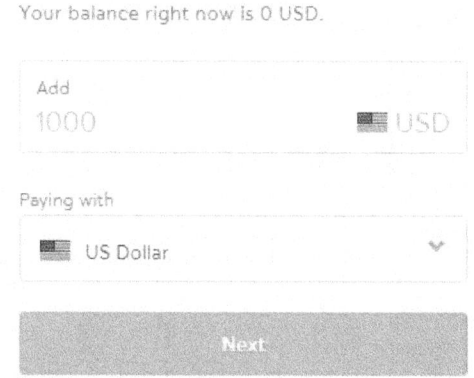

It also applies for GBP Account.

Another way to top-up money is by inviting your friends to use TransferWise services.

Go to menu "Invite & earn 50 GBP" and send the personal link to your friends by Whatsapp, Facebook Messenger, Posting to Facebook and Tweeter.

Once you manage to invite 3 friends and each of them make a qualifying payment of at least 200 GBP each then you'll get 50 GBP as a reward

CHAPTER 10 - TRANSFERWISE FEES

So what about the fees ? How much TransferWise charge for their services ?

So far, it seems they charged very little for their services

But let's see what they say in their website

For using their Account related services

Account pricing	
Creating your account	Free
Hold 40+ currency balances	Free
Get a UK account number and sort code	Free
Get a U.S. routing and wiring number	Free
Get a European IBAN	Free
Get an Australian account and BSB number	Free
Get a New Zealand account number	Free
Fixed fee to send money (varies by currency)	65p
Receive money in EUR, USD, GBP, PLN, AUD & NZD	Free

For using their Debit Card services

Card pricing	
Spend in currencies in your account	Free
Convert a currency using your card	See price checker
ATM withdrawals up to £200 / 30 days	Free
ATM withdrawals over £200 / 30 days	2%

So it seems they only charge when there's a currency conversion, add money to an account and send money from balance

CHAPTER 11 - WITHDRAW MONEY FROM TRANSFERWISE

Withdrawing money is quite simple. The idea is to send money to yourself

However, before you can do that, you need to add your local bank account as a recipient

1. Go to "Recipients" menu
2. Click on "Add your bank account" button

It will open a new window where you can enter the details of your local bank account

1. Still in "Recipient" menu
2. Choose your Bank Account then click on "Send Money" button

You will be prompted to enter the amount

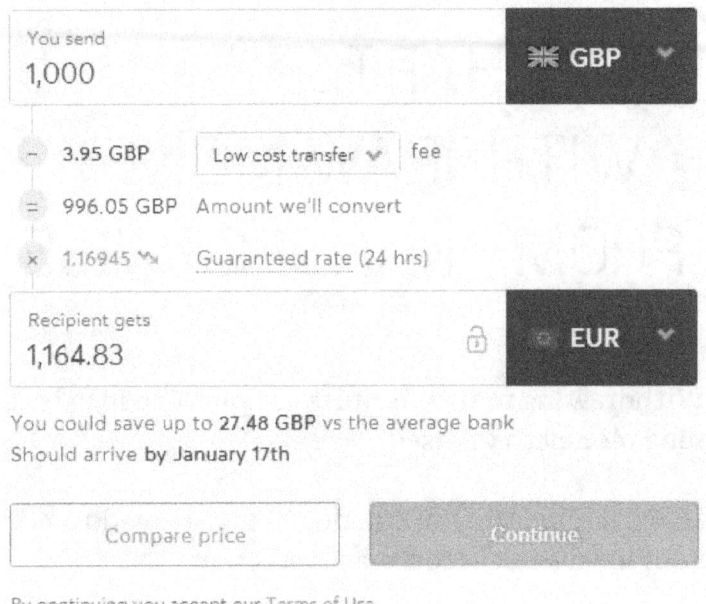

Once you click Continue, they will ask you the reason for your transfer

What's the reason for your transfer?

To help us keep TransferWise safe and secure, please let us know why you're making this transfer.

Reason for your transfer

Select a reason...   ▼

Continue

Once finished, you only need to review and click "Confirm and Continue"

Another way to Withdraw Money is by using a Debit Card provided by TransferWise.

Unfortunately, it's not available to some countries.

CHAPTER 12 – CONCLUSION

There are pros and cons when you consider the option to use Payoneer or TransferWise

TransferWise has some cheaper fees and supported lots more currencies compare to Payoneer but Payoneer provided Debit Card to most countries so their users have the option to withdraw Payoneer's balances from ATMs

So instead of choosing just one of them, why not sign up for both Payoneer and TransferWise ?

ABOUT THE AUTHOR

Anok Polemos is a writer / blogger that loves travelling, reading and also a technology-enthusiasts that sometimes dwell into programming as well.